7 Weeks Guide To Overcoming

BREAKUP

Grief For Women

Interactive Workbook for Healing from Abusive Relationships and Surviving Difficult Separations

Lucy J. Brainly

Disclaimer

This book is designed to be a supportive companion on your path to healing from an abusive relationship. And guide you through self-discovery, foster self-compassion, and empower you to move forward with strength.

It's critical to keep in mind that individual outcomes and experiences may differ.

DEDICATION

Dedicated to the countless women who choose to rewrite their stories. This workbook is for you, the one who dared to walk away from a love that stole your light.

Let the healing begin, not with overcoming, but with embracing the journey. You are not alone.

Here's to rediscovering your voice, rebuilding a life filled with joy, and leaving the shadows of the past behind. You are a survivor, and your resilience is a beacon of hope for others.

This workbook is your companion, a witness to your strength, and a testament to the incredible woman you are becoming.

ACKNOWLEDGEMENT

This workbook wasn't born in a flash of inspiration, but rather emerged from the quiet whispers of countless stories. It's a culmination of late nights spent reading journals and articles penned by brave women who shared their experiences with heartbreak and resilience.

Their voices became the guiding light, leading me to weave together a path towards healing.

A deep gratitude goes out to the experts in the field of trauma and recovery – their research and insights formed the foundation of this book.

Your constant encouragement fueled my passion and kept me focused on the bigger picture – empowering women to reclaim their lives.

WHY THIS BOOK?

This breakup workbook isn't a one-size-fits-all approach. It's specifically designed for women who have experienced the trauma of an abusive relationship.

It recognizes the unique challenges you face and provides targeted exercises, journaling prompts, and expert insights to help you on your healing journey.

Here's what you can achieve with this book:

1. Learn to recognize the manipulative tactics used in abusive relationships and develop healthy boundaries to protect yourself from future harm.

2. Gain tools and strategies for coping with anger, guilt, fear, and other emotions that often arise after an abusive breakup.

3. This workbook will guide you through exercises to cultivate self-love, appreciate your strengths, and silence the inner critic.

4. Learn to set clear boundaries and red flags to identify and avoid unhealthy dynamics in future relationships.

5. This book empowers you to discover your inner strength, rebuild your confidence, and move towards a brighter future.

"Overcoming Breakup Grief for Women" is more than just a workbook. It's a supportive companion on your path to healing, offering a safe space to process your experiences, celebrate your progress, and discover the joy you deserve.

HOW TO USE THIS WORKBOOK

1. Dedicate a quiet space for your workbook sessions. This could be a cozy corner in your bedroom, a park bench under a calming tree, or anywhere you feel comfortable and secure.

2. Have a pen, some colorful markers or highlighters (optional), and a box of tissues (because healing can involve tears, and that's okay!).

3. This workbook is structured with a week-by-week approach. Each week focuses on a specific theme related to healing from abuse.

4. Schedule time for your workbook sessions at least 3-4 times a week.

5. This workbook offers a variety of activities and exercises to help you break down complex emotions, challenge negative thought patterns, and build resilience.

These activities can be done independently or incorporated into your journaling practice.

6. Each week concludes with a check-in section. Reflect on your progress, celebrate your achievements, and acknowledge any areas where you might need additional support.

Remember!

There's no "right" or "wrong" way to use this workbook. Go at your own pace, revisit specific sections as needed, and don't hesitate to adapt the prompts or activities to fit your unique journey.

TABLE OF CONTENT

INTRODUCTION

Breakups. The very word evokes a storm of emotions; sadness, anger, confusion, and sometimes even relief. It's a universal human experience, a necessary pruning of the emotional garden to allow space for new growth. But let's be honest, the pruning shears can feel awfully sharp in the moment.

The very word evokes a storm of emotions; sadness, anger, confusion, and sometimes even relief. It's a universal human experience, a necessary pruning of the emotional garden to allow space for new growth. But let's be honest, the pruning shears can feel awfully sharp in the moment.

In actuality, you're stuck till you let go, forgive yourself, forgive the other person, and learn from the circumstance. You're stuck in a situation that's not even there anymore. And that's not a good place to be.

Especially when the relationship ended on a difficult note, the road to healing can seem daunting, an endless stretch of gray skies and tear-stained cheeks.

But what if I told you that within ten weeks, you could be standing on the other side, not unscathed perhaps, but stronger, wiser, and ready to embrace a brighter future?

This book isn't a magic bullet. It won't make the heartbreak disappear overnight. But it is a guided compass, a supportive hand in the darkness, a roadmap to help you navigate the often-turbulent terrain of post-breakup healing – especially if the relationship was abusive or particularly difficult.

Here's the truth – you are more resilient than you think. You've weathered this storm before, and you will again. This breakup, no matter how painful, is not the end of your story.

It's a turning point, a chance to rewrite the narrative, to reclaim your power, and to build a life that truly reflects your values and desires.

Common Signs of an Abusive Relationship:

1. Constant criticism and put-downs: Your partner consistently undermines your confidence, belittles your achievements, and makes you feel worthless.

2. Controlling behavior: Your partner dictates who you see, what you wear, and how you spend your time. They might monitor your phone, isolate you from friends and family, or use guilt trips to get their way.

3. Emotional manipulation: Your partner makes you feel like you're "crazy" or overreacting. They might threaten you, gaslight you (deny or twist reality), or use guilt to control your emotions.

4. Threats and intimidation: Your partner threatens physical violence, makes you feel unsafe, or destroys your belongings.

If any of these red flags resonate with you, know this – you are not alone. Millions of people suffer through abusive relationships. But you don't have to be a victim.

You have the power to break free and build a life filled with love, respect, and happiness.

But where do you even begin?

The first step is acknowledging the pain. It's okay to feel everything – the crushing sadness, the white-hot anger, the paralyzing fear.

Ignoring or suppressing these emotions will only prolong the healing process. Instead, let yourself feel. Cry until the tears dry up. Scream into a pillow (just maybe not at 3 am when your neighbors are trying to sleep). Write angry letters you'll never send.

This isn't about wallowing. It's about acknowledging the depth of your emotions and allowing them a safe space to exist.

Once you've acknowledged the pain, it's time to start taking care of yourself. This is not a time for self-deprecation or neglect. You've been through a battle, and your emotional reserves are depleted. Now is the time to be gentle with yourself, to nurture your body, mind, and spirit.

Prioritize sleep. Eat healthy meals, even if it's just a smoothie or a bowl of cereal. Even a quick stroll around the block counts as regular exercise.

Reconnect with activities that bring you joy, whether it's reading, painting, spending time in nature, or listening to music.

Surround yourself with supportive loved ones who will listen without judgment and offer comfort and encouragement.

Remember, you are not alone. Millions of people have walked this path before you, and millions more will walk it after.

Lean on your support system. Talk to friends, family, or a therapist. Make yourself known to others by joining a support group for victims of abuse.

Breaking free from an abusive relationship requires not just emotional healing but also rebuilding a sense of safety and trust.

This is where the guided journal prompts in this book will become your invaluable companion. Journaling is a powerful tool for self-discovery and emotional processing.

It allows you to explore your feelings in a safe space, to identify patterns and triggers, and to gain clarity on your needs and desires for future relationships.

The prompts within these pages will guide you through various exercises, from acknowledging the pain of the breakup to identifying your strengths and setting healthy boundaries.

There will be days when the exercises feel overwhelming, and days when you don't feel like picking up a pen. That's okay. Be gentle with yourself. This is a journey, not a race.

Remember, the goal isn't to erase the past or pretend everything is okay. It's about learning from your experiences, forgiving yourself and your ex (if that feels right for you), and moving forward with newfound strength and confidence.

This journey of healing isn't linear. There will be setbacks, days when you feel like you've taken ten steps back. But don't let that discourage you. See those setbacks as temporary detours, not roadblocks. Each time you pick yourself up and continue moving forward, you become a little bit stronger, a little bit more resilient.

And slowly, but surely, the fog will begin to lift. You'll start to see the world in brighter colors again. You'll rediscover your passions and dreams.

You'll start to feel a glimmer of hope for the future, a future where you are whole, empowered, and ready to embrace love that is healthy, respectful, and fulfilling.

This ten-week program is designed to be a springboard for your healing, a catalyst for personal growth. Each week will focus on a specific aspect of the healing journey, with journaling prompts, self-reflection exercises, and practical tips to guide you along the way.

Week 1: Processing the Pain

This first week is all about acknowledging the pain of the breakup. The world feels shattered, and you might be wondering how you'll ever pick up the pieces. Allow yourself to feel the full spectrum of emotions – sadness, anger, confusion, even relief. Journaling prompts will help you explore these emotions and begin to understand their root causes.

Week 2: Self-Compassion and Support

After acknowledging the pain, it's time to focus on self-compassion. You've been through a difficult experience, and you deserve kindness and understanding. This week will be about nourishing your body, mind, and spirit.

Week 3: Releasing the Past

Letting go of the past can be a challenging yet crucial step in healing. This week will focus on processing the anger, hurt, and resentment you might be harboring towards your ex.

Week 4: Building Your Resilience

Breakups can take a toll on your self-esteem. This week will focus on identifying your strengths and rebuilding your sense of self-worth.

Week 5: Rebuilding Your Life

Breakups can leave you feeling lost and unsure of your future. This week will be about rediscovering your passions and setting goals for the future you want to create.

Week 7: Dating Again (if you're ready)

While some people might jump back into dating right away, others might need more time to heal. This week will focus on preparing yourself for healthy dating in the future, whenever you feel ready.

Week 8: Celebrating Your Victories

Healing is a journey, not a destination. This week will be about celebrating your progress, no matter how small it may seem.

Remember, healing is a nonlinear process. There will be good days and bad days. But with each passing week, you'll become stronger, more resilient, and more confident. You'll rediscover the incredible person you are, and you'll be ready to embrace the love and happiness you deserve.

WEEK 1: PROCESSING THE PAIN

The heart was made to be broken. While undeniably poetic, that statement does little to capture the raw, gut-wrenching pain of a fresh breakup. It feels less like your heart is broken and more like it's been ripped from your chest, stomped on, and left for dead on the emotional sidewalk.

Statistics back this up. Studies show that breakups can trigger a cascade of physiological and emotional changes, mimicking the very real experience of withdrawal from addictive drugs. The brain's reward system, accustomed to the dopamine rush of a loving relationship, goes into overdrive, craving the comfort and security it once provided.

This can manifest as intense emotional pain, anxiety, and even physical symptoms like fatigue and difficulty sleeping. But here's the good news: even the most excruciating breakups don't have to be the end of your story. This first week of our Breakup Bootcamp is dedicated to acknowledging and processing the pain, a crucial step in your healing journey.

Facing the Feels

Trying to ignore or suppress your emotions after a breakup is like trying to hold a beach ball underwater. It might work for a while, but eventually, it's going to pop up with a vengeance.

So, this week, we're giving you permission to feel everything – the crushing sadness, the white-hot anger, the paralyzing fear. Cry until the tears dry up. Write angry letters you'll never send.

Don't compare your experience to others'. Some people need to completely withdraw and process their emotions in private, while others find solace in talking to friends or family. Honor your own needs and create a safe space for yourself to express your pain.

Here are some activities that might help you process your emotions:

• **Journaling:** Use this week's journaling prompts to explore the full spectrum of your emotions.

• **Creative Expression:** If words fail you, turn to art, music, or dance to express your emotions.

• **Talking it Out:** Find a supportive friend, family member, or therapist to talk to. Vocalizing your pain can provide a sense of relief and validation.

• Movement: Exercise releases endorphins, those feel-good chemicals in your brain that can help combat depression and anxiety. Go for a walk, run, dance class, or anything that gets your body moving.

• **Beyond the Tears:** The Power of Self-Compassion

While acknowledging the pain is vital, wallowing isn't. This week is also about cultivating self-compassion.

You wouldn't berate a friend going through a difficult time, so why do it to yourself? Treat yourself with the same kindness and understanding you'd offer a loved one.

Ways to Practice Self-compassion

• **Positive Self-Talk:** Replace negative self-talk with affirmations like "I am strong," "I am worthy of love," and "I will get through this."

- **Mindfulness:** Practice mindfulness techniques like meditation or deep breathing to become more aware of your thoughts and feelings without judgment.

- **Nourishing Activities:** Focus on nourishing your body, mind, and spirit. Eat healthy foods, get regular sleep, and engage in activities that bring you joy.

Remember, You Are Not Alone

Breakups are a universal human experience. Millions of people have walked this path before you, and millions more will walk it after.

This week, lean on your support system. Reach out to friends, family, or a therapist who can offer comfort and encouragement. Consider joining a support group for survivors of abusive relationships if your experience was marked by abuse.

This first week might be the toughest, but it's also the most important. By acknowledging your pain and practicing self-compassion, you're laying the foundation for your healing journey. Remember, the sun will rise again, and you will too.

This week's journey isn't about pretending everything is okay. It's about acknowledging the storm within and taking the first courageous step towards calmer waters. Keep going, one tear, one breath, one kind word to yourself at a time. I am with you on this journey.

Week 1 Journaling Prompts

Write a letter to your ex, expressing all the emotions you're feeling - the hurt, the anger, the confusion.

Remember, this is just for you, and you don't have to send it!

Remember, this is just for you, and you don't have to send it!

MY THOUGHTS

My Thoughts

WEEK 2: SELF-COMPASSION AND SUPPORT

The pain of the breakup might be compounded by lingering feelings of betrayal hurt, and a deep-seated sense of injustice.

This week of Breakup Bootcamp focuses on self-compassion and building a strong support system, crucial elements for healing from any breakup, but especially important for survivors of abuse.

The Gift of Self-Compassion

After enduring the emotional rollercoaster of an abusive relationship, it's easy to fall into a trap of self-blame and negativity.

You might replay arguments in your head, wondering what you could have done differently. You might question your judgment and your worth as a person.

But here's the truth – you are not to blame for the abuse. It's essential to understand that abusive behavior is a choice made by the abuser, not a consequence of your actions or inactions.

This week, I am challenging you to cultivate self-compassion. Imagine treating a dear friend who just went through a similar experience.

You wouldn't berate them, would you?

You'd offer them love, support, and a listening ear. Extend the same kindness and understanding to yourself.

Building Your Support System

No one heals in isolation. This week, focus on building a strong support system – a network of people who love, support, and believe in you. These could be friends, family members, a therapist, or even a support group for survivors of abuse. Never hesitate to seek for assistance. Sharing your stories with others can be a very effective healing strategy.

Strategies for Expanding Your Network of Support

• Connect with Friends and Family: Lean on loved ones who offer a safe space for you to express your emotions without judgment.

• Consider Therapy: A therapist can provide professional guidance and support as you navigate the healing process.

• Join a Support Group: Connecting with others who have been through similar experiences can be incredibly validating and empowering. Support groups can also offer practical advice and coping mechanisms.

Boundaries: Protecting Yourself

If your relationship was marked by abuse, rebuilding trust can be challenging. This week, we'll also begin to explore the concept of boundaries – healthy limits you set in your relationships to protect yourself from emotional harm.

Here are some initial thoughts on boundaries:

1. Identify Your Needs: Take time to reflect on your emotional and physical needs. What kind of treatment do you deserve in a relationship?

2. Communicate Your Needs: Once you understand your needs, learn to communicate them clearly and assertively to others.

3. Enforce Your Boundaries: Setting boundaries is just the first step. It's equally important to enforce them, even if it means walking away from unhealthy situations or people.

Remember, building a strong support system and setting healthy boundaries are ongoing processes.

This week is about taking the first steps and planting the seeds for a future filled with healthy, supportive relationships.

This week of Breakup Bootcamp is about self-care and building a foundation for healing.

By practicing self-compassion, reaching out for support, and setting healthy boundaries, you're taking back control of your life and creating the space for healthier relationships in the future.

Week 2 Journaling Prompts

Write a letter to your future self, offering words of comfort and
encouragement.

Remember, this is just for you, and you don't have to send it!

Remember, this is just for you, and you don't have to send it!

Week 2 Journaling Prompts

What advice would you give yourself right now, knowing what you know?

____

____

____

____

____

____

____

____

____

____

____

____

Remember, this is just for you, and you don't have to send it!

Remember, this is just for you, and you don't have to send it!

Week 2 Journaling Prompts

Reflect on your support system. Who are the people you can rely on for love and support? How can you strengthen these connections?

Ask for the love and support you deserve. You are worth it.

Ask for the love and support you deserve. You are worth it.

My strengths

My Positive Qualities.

Ask for the love and support you deserve. You are worth it.

WEEK 3: LETTING GO OF THE PAST

While the pain of the past might still linger, this week is about taking ownership of your present and future. We'll focus on letting go of the past, not in the sense of erasing memories, but rather in releasing the emotional grip they hold on you.

The Power of Forgiveness

Forgiveness is often a misunderstood concept, especially for survivors of abuse. It doesn't mean condoning the abuser's actions or minimizing the pain they inflicted.

Forgiveness is about releasing yourself from the emotional burden of anger and resentment. It's about freeing yourself to move forward with an open heart.

Here's why forgiveness is crucial for healing:

• Letting Go of Anger: Holding onto anger is like drinking poison and expecting the other person to get sick. Forgiveness allows you to release the negativity and reclaim your emotional well-being.

• Breaking the Cycle: Abuse thrives on power and control. Forgiveness takes away the power the abuser holds over your emotions.

• Moving Forward: True healing can't happen while you're stuck in the past. Forgiveness allows you to close that chapter and move on to a brighter future.

The process of forgiveness is personal and may take time.

The following tips will be useful to you:

• Acknowledge Your Pain: Before you can forgive, you need to acknowledge the hurt you've experienced.

• Set Boundaries: Forgiveness doesn't mean reconciliation. You can forgive someone from a distance and choose to have no further contact with them.

• Focus on Yourself: The goal of forgiveness is your own healing and well-being.

Letting Go Doesn't Mean Forgetting. Letting go of the past doesn't mean erasing the memories of your relationship.

Those experiences, both positive and negative, have shaped you into the person you are today. The goal is to learn from the past and use those lessons to build a brighter future.

Strategies for Letting Go:

• Limit Contact: If possible, minimize contact with your ex and avoid places or activities that might trigger painful memories.

• Release Mementos: Consider putting away photos, mementos, or gifts that evoke negative emotions. You can revisit them later when you're in a stronger emotional space, or choose to discard them altogether.

• Reframe Memories: Try to reframe negative memories in a more empowering light. What self-discovery did you get from the experience? How did it make you stronger?

Embrace the Power of Now

This week, challenge yourself to be fully present in the here and now. Savor the simple joys in life, the warmth of the sun on your skin, the laughter of a friend, the beauty of a blooming flower.

Here are some ways to cultivate mindfulness:

• Practice Gratitude: Take time each day to reflect on the things you're grateful for, big or small.

• Get Involved with Your Senses: Observe the sights, sounds, tastes, scents, and textures nearby.

• Mindfulness Exercises: Consider incorporating meditation or deep breathing exercises into your daily routine.

There will be good days and bad days. But by practicing forgiveness, embracing the present moment, and focusing on your future, you'll gradually loosen the grip of the past and create space for new beginnings.

Week 3 Journaling Prompts

Write a letter to your anger. Express your frustration, hurt, and resentment.

Remember, this is for you, not necessarily for the abuser

Remember, this is for you, not necessarily for the abuser

Week 3 Journaling Prompts

Write a letter of forgiveness.

Remember, this is for you, not necessarily for the abuser

Remember, this is for you, not necessarily for the abuser

Week 3 Journaling Prompts

What qualities did you possess that helped you through that experience?
How can you tap into those strengths again as you move forward?

Remember, this is for you, not necessarily for the abuser

Remember, this is for you, not necessarily for the abuser

Vision Board

My Goals

My Dreams

Ask for the love and support you deserve. You are worth it.

My Desires

Notes

Ask for the love and support you deserve. You are worth it.

WEEK 4: BUILDING YOUR EMOTIONAL RESILIENCE

Just like the willow tree that bends but doesn't break in the face of a storm, emotion resilience is the ability to adapt to life's challenges and bounce back from adversity.

This week of Breakup Bootcamp is dedicated to building your emotional resilience, a crucial skill not just for healing from your breakup but for thriving in life. Here's why emotional resilience is so important:

• Reduced Stress and Anxiety: Resilient people are better equipped to manage stress and anxiety, leading to a greater sense of well-being.

• Faster Recovery: Life inevitably throws curveballs. Emotional resilience allows you to recover from setbacks more quickly and move forward with a positive outlook.

• Increased Confidence: As you overcome challenges and bounce back from setbacks, your confidence grows, empowering you to take risks and pursue your goals.

The Pillars of Resilience

Emotional resilience isn't a single trait, but rather a combination of skills and characteristics. Here are some key pillars to focus on this week:

• Positive Mindset: Cultivate a positive outlook. Have faith in your own abilities and your capacity to overcome obstacles.

• Healthy Coping Mechanisms: Develop healthy ways to manage stress, such as exercise, relaxation techniques, or creative expression.

• Strong Support System: Surround yourself with positive and supportive people who uplift and encourage you.

• Self-Compassion: Treat yourself with kindness and understanding. Don't beat yourself up for setbacks.

Building Your Positive Mindset

Our thoughts significantly impact our emotions and actions. This week, we'll focus on developing a more positive and growth-oriented mindset.

Techniques:

• Challenge Negative Thoughts: When you catch yourself engaging in negative self-talk, challenge those thoughts and replace them with more empowering beliefs.

• Practice Gratitude: Taking time each day to reflect on the things you're grateful for, big or small, can significantly boost your mood and overall well-being.

• Focus on the Present: Ruminating on the past or worrying about the future can drain your energy. Practice mindfulness techniques to stay present in the here and now.

Developing Healthy Coping Mechanisms

Everyone experiences stress and difficult emotions. The key is having healthy ways to manage them. Here are some strategies to explore this week:

• Workout: Being physically active is a great way to decompress. Find an exercise routine you enjoy, whether it's dancing, running, swimming, or yoga.

• Relaxation Methods: You can relax your body and mind by using methods like progressive muscle relaxation, deep breathing, and meditation.

• Creative Expression: Writing, painting, music, or any other form of creative expression can be a healthy way to release pent-up emotions.

Building emotional resilience is an ongoing process. This week is about planting the seeds and developing the tools you need to navigate life's challenges with greater strength and flexibility.

Remember, rise above your past, build your resilience, and create a future filled with hope and possibility.

Week 4 Journaling Prompts

Identify your negative self-talk patterns. What are some critical thoughts you tell yourself frequently? Challenge those thoughts and rewrite them in a more positive and empowering light.

Remember, this is for you, not necessarily for the abuser

Week 4 Journaling Prompts

Reflect on a challenging experience from your past. How can you utilize those strategies again in the future?

Remember, this is for you, not necessarily for the abuser

My Gratitude List

This could be anything from your health and loved ones to a beautiful sunset or a delicious cup of coffee.

Ask for the love and support you deserve. You are worth it.

My strengths

My Positive Qualities.

Ask for the love and support you deserve. You are worth it.

WEEK 5: REBUILDING YOUR LIFE

A STORY ABOUT AMELIA

Rain lashed against the windowpane, mirroring the storm raging inside **Amelia**. Five weeks. Five agonizing weeks since **Michael** had walked out, leaving behind a gaping hole in her life and a heart fractured beyond repair.

Their three-year relationship, a whirlwind of passionate highs punctuated by confusing lows, had finally imploded, leaving Amelia questioning everything she thought she knew about love.

The initial weeks were a blur of tear-stained tissues, unanswered calls, and the suffocating silence of their once-shared apartment. Memories, both cherished and painful, played on repeat in her mind. The first stolen kiss under the fairy lights in a Parisian cafe, the cruel sting of his words during a heated argument, the hollow promises whispered in the dead of night.

This week, however, felt different. A sliver of sunlight, faint but persistent, peeked through the storm clouds in Amelia's heart.

Week 5 of Breakup Bootcamp had a different focus – Rebuilding Your Life. It felt daunting, like trying to rebuild a sandcastle after a relentless tide. But a tiny spark of defiance flickered within her. Maybe, just maybe, she could salvage the pieces and create something new, something stronger.

The past few weeks had been a journey of self-discovery. She'd reconnected with old friends, the ones who'd faded away during the all-consuming intensity of her relationship with Michael.

Laughter filled the air once more, genuine and unburdened. She'd unearthed a passion for painting she'd neglected for years, the vibrant colors a stark contrast to the emotional grayscale she'd been living in.

This week, however, the focus shifted outwards. This book challenged her to confront the physical remnants of the relationship – the framed photos gathering dust on the bookshelf, the half-read novel they'd planned to finish together, the worn t-shirt that still held the faint scent of his cologne. Each item held a memory, a bittersweet pang in her heart.

Amelia spent the afternoon sorting through these relics. Some photos, the ones that captured genuine joy, were tucked into a box labeled "Memories." The rest, the ones that evoked a grimace or a tear, were placed in a separate box for a future garage sale, a symbolic letting go. The t-shirt, after a moment of hesitation, joined the donation pile.

As the sun began to set, casting an orange glow across the room, Amelia stood amidst the remnants of her past. A sense of accomplishment washed over her. It wasn't a complete overhaul, but a small step towards reclaiming her space, her life.

The book also encouraged her to reconnect with the world outside her apartment. It suggested volunteering for a cause she cared about, taking a dance class, or simply exploring a new part of town. The idea of salsa dancing, something she'd always wanted to try but dismissed as "silly," sparked a flicker of excitement.

The next day, Amelia found herself standing nervously outside a brightly lit dance studio.

The instructor, a woman with a warm smile and infectious energy, welcomed Amelia with open arms. The first few steps were awkward, her feet stumbling over the unfamiliar rhythm. But as the music continued, a strange thing happened. Amelia started to relax, letting the music guide her movements. Her worries about Michael, the pain of the breakup, faded into the background.

For the first time in weeks, she felt a genuine smile bloom on her face. It wasn't a forced smile plastered on to mask the hurt, but a genuine expression of joy in the simple act of moving her body to the music. As the class ended, Amelia walked out of the studio feeling lighter, a newfound sense of possibility swirling around her.

Week 5 wasn't about forgetting the past or erasing Michael from her life. It was about acknowledging the pain, learning from the experience, and taking the first steps towards rebuilding a life that reflected her true self, a life filled with laughter, passion, and the exhilarating uncertainty of new beginnings.

The storm within Amelia might not have completely subsided, but the sun had finally broken through the clouds, casting a hopeful light on the path ahead.

This week, she wasn't just surviving the breakup; she was starting to thrive.

Amelia's story might have resonated with you in a multitude of ways.

Perhaps you, too, have recently emerged from a relationship that left you feeling emotionally battered and questioning your own worth. Maybe the manipulative tactics and emotional abuse Michael inflicted on Amelia mirror experiences you've had in your own past. Or perhaps, you simply recognize the universal pain of heartbreak and the daunting task of rebuilding your life after a significant loss.

Regardless of your specific circumstances, Amelia's journey offers valuable life lessons and takeaways that can empower you on your own healing path.

Life Lessons:

1. Breakups are a Process, Not an Event: Healing doesn't happen overnight. It's a journey with ups and downs, moments of intense grief followed by periods of newfound strength. Acknowledge your emotions, don't suppress them.

2. Self-Compassion is Key: Treat yourself with the same kindness and understanding you'd offer a friend going through a similar experience. Forgive yourself for past mistakes and focus on building yourself back up.

3. The Power of Support: Don't isolate yourself. Surround yourself with loved ones who offer unwavering support and a listening ear. Consider therapy or joining a support group for survivors of abuse.

4. Reclaim Your Life: Don't let the past define you. Rediscover your passions, explore new interests, and reconnect with the parts of yourself that might have been neglected during the relationship.

5. Taking Action is Empowering: Small steps like sorting through memories, trying a new activity, or simply venturing out into the world can make a big difference in your healing journey.

Key Takeaways:

1. You are not alone: Millions of people experience breakups, and countless others have survived abusive relationships. There is support available, and your sorrow is legitimate.

2. Healing takes time: Be patient with yourself. There will be good days and bad days. No matter how little the development appears to be, keep your attention on it.

3. Your strength lies within: You are capable of overcoming this. Draw on your inner resilience and the support system you've built around you.

4. This is an opportunity for growth: This experience can make you stronger, wiser, and more self-aware. Let it guide you towards creating healthier, more fulfilling relationships in the future.

5. The future is yours to create: The heartbreak might linger, but so does the possibility of love, joy, and a life that reflects your true self. Embrace the unknown and step into the future with hope and optimism.

Remember, healing is a journey, not a destination. There will be setbacks along the way, but with self-compassion, a strong support system, and a commitment to growth, you can emerge from this experience stronger, more resilient, and ready to embrace the love and happiness that awaits you.

What are some of the negative self-talk patterns I've developed as a result of the relationship? How can I challenge those thoughts and replace them with more empowering beliefs?

Who are the people in my life who offer me unconditional love and support?
How can I strengthen these connections?

Self-Reflection Questions:

What are some of my passions that I might have neglected during the relationship? How can I make time for them again?

____

____

____

____

____

____

____

____

____

____

____

____

What are some small, concrete steps I can take this week to reclaim my life and move forward?

Self-Reflection Questions:

What are some of the lessons I've learned from this experience? How can I use them to create healthier relationships in the future?

WEEK 6: NAVIGATING THE DATING SCENE AGAIN

Six weeks since Michael's departure, six weeks since the world as she knew it had fractured. The initial weeks had been a blur of tear-stained tissues and suffocating loneliness. But the past few weeks had been different.

Week 5, "Rebuilding Your Life," had been a turning point. Reconnecting with old friends, rediscovering her passion for painting, and the exhilarating liberation of salsa dancing had chipped away at the walls of grief. She wasn't healed, not completely, but a flicker of hope had ignited within her.

Week 6 of Breakup Bootcamp, however, presented a new challenge – "Navigating the Dating Scene Again." The mere thought sent a jolt of anxiety through her.

Was she ready?

Was there a part of her that even wanted to be ready?

Memories of awkward first dates with Michael, the forced smiles and nervous small talk, played on repeat in her mind. The vulnerability of opening her heart again, the possibility of getting hurt all over again, felt daunting. Yet, a tiny voice whispered a question – could love, real, healthy love, exist after the wreckage of her past relationship?

The book offered a gentle nudge, suggesting she ease back into the dating scene slowly, focusing on casual interactions rather than immediate commitment. It emphasized the importance of setting boundaries and prioritizing her own well-being.

Amelia decided to start small. She signed up for a local book club, a safe space to meet new people who shared her love of literature. The first meeting was a whirlwind of introductions, nervous laughter, and lively discussions.

There was Daniel, a kind-eyed history professor with a passion for obscure French poetry. There was Sarah, a witty accountant with a penchant for detective novels. And then there was Ethan, a quiet musician with a shy smile and an aura of mystery.

Over the following weeks, Amelia found herself drawn to Ethan's quiet intensity. He listened intently as she shared stories of her past, both the happy and the heartbreaking. He never pressured her, respected her boundaries, and made her laugh with his dry wit.

One evening, after a particularly engaging book club discussion, Ethan walked Amelia home. As they strolled under the starlit sky, a comfortable silence settled between them. He stopped abruptly, his gaze meeting hers.

"You have incredible strength," he said, his voice soft. "The way you're healing, rebuilding your life... it's inspiring."

Amelia's heart stuttered. It was the first time someone had acknowledged the emotional journey she'd been on. Tears welled up in her eyes, a mixture of gratitude and vulnerability.

Ethan reached out, wiping a stray tear with his thumb. "Can I kiss you?" he asked, his voice barely a whisper.

The question hung in the air, a silent invitation. Amelia hesitated, a million doubts swirling in her mind. But then, something shifted within her. A tiny spark of defiance, a flicker of hope.

Taking a deep breath, Amelia met his gaze. "Yes," she whispered, the single word laced with a newfound courage.

The kiss was tender, a hesitant exploration. It wasn't fireworks or earth-shattering passion, but a slow burn, a promise of something genuine and new.

As they pulled away, Amelia felt a warmth bloom in her chest, a feeling she hadn't experienced in months – the possibility of connection, of love that felt safe and respectful. This wasn't about replacing Michael, it was about creating something new, something built on a foundation of honesty, communication, and mutual respect.

The road ahead might hold uncertainties, but for the first time in a long time, Amelia didn't feel alone on the journey.

She had the strength of her own healing, the support of her loved ones, and the possibility of a future filled with love and happiness.

Week 6 wasn't just about dating again; it was about opening her heart to the possibility of love, a love that was healthy, supportive, and deserving of the incredible woman she was becoming.

Amelia's story might resonate with you in a powerful way if you're contemplating re-entering the dating scene after a breakup, especially one marked by emotional abuse. Perhaps you, too, are grappling with the fear of vulnerability and the possibility of getting hurt again. Maybe the memories of unhealthy past relationships leave you questioning your ability to find true love.

Regardless of your specific circumstances, Amelia's journey offers valuable life lessons and takeaways that can empower you to approach dating with a healthy dose of caution and a hopeful heart.

Life Lessons:

1. Healing is a Prerequisite for Healthy Relationships: Don't jump back into dating to fill a void or numb the pain of your past relationship.

Take time to heal, process your emotions, and rebuild your self-esteem.

2. Setting Boundaries is Essential: Know your worth and what you deserve in a partner. Set clear boundaries regarding acceptable behavior and don't settle for anything less than respect and kindness.

3. Start Small and Prioritize Safety: Ease back into the dating scene gradually, perhaps through social settings or group activities, before venturing into one-on-one dates. Suable life lessons and takeaways that can empower you to approach dating with a healthy dose of caution and a hopeful heart.

4. Listen to Your Intuition: Pay attention to your gut feeling. If something feels off about a potential partner, trust your instincts and walk away.

5. Focus on Compatibility, Not Just Chemistry: Look for someone who shares your values, respects your boundaries, and supports your personal growth.

Key Takeaways:

1. You Deserve Healthy Love: The love you experienced in your past relationship might not have been healthy, but that doesn't mean true love doesn't exist. You deserve a partner who cherishes you, respects you, and supports your growth.

2. Healing Takes Time: Be patient with yourself. The wounds of your past relationship might take time to heal completely. That's okay.

3. Your Past Doesn't Define Your Future: The challenges you've overcome have made you stronger and wiser. Let them guide you towards creating healthier relationships in the future.

4. Opening Your Heart is a Risk, But Worth It: Love is always a risk, but it's a risk worth taking. By approaching dating with caution and a healthy dose of self-love, you increase your chances of finding a fulfilling and lasting connection.

5. You Are Not Alone: Millions of people navigate the post-breakup dating scene. There are resources and support groups available to help you on your journey.

Practice Self-Compassion

Write a letter to yourself acknowledging your strength and resilience in overcoming your past relationship.

Self-Reflection Questions:

What are my emotional triggers when it comes to dating? How can I manage these triggers in a healthy way?

____

____

____

____

____

____

____

____

____

____

____

____

____

Self-Reflection Questions:

What are my non-negotiables in a relationship? What are my dealbreakers?

Self-Reflection Questions:

Am I truly ready to open my heart to someone new, or am I using dating as a distraction from unresolved emotions?

Self-Reflection Questions:

What are some of the unhealthy relationship patterns I might be unconsciously repeating?

Self-Reflection Questions:

What are my hopes and dreams for a future relationship?

WEEK 7: CELEBRATING YOUR VICTORIES AND MOVING FORWARD

Amelia kicked at a fallen leaf, a bittersweet smile gracing her lips. Seven weeks. Seven weeks since the world as she knew it had been turned upside down.

The past few weeks had been a whirlwind of emotions – grief, anger, self-discovery, and a newfound sense of hope. Week 7 of Breakup Bootcamp was titled "Celebrating Your Victories and Moving Forward." At first, the idea of celebrating victories felt a bit foreign.

What victories were there to celebrate amidst the wreckage of her relationship?

But as she delved deeper into the exercises, a shift began to occur. The book encouraged her to reflect on how far she'd come. She could now navigate the grocery store without reaching for the familiar brand Michael preferred.

She'd reconnected with old friends, their laughter a soothing balm on her wounded spirit. And most importantly, she'd begun to trust herself again, her intuition guiding her towards a future filled with possibility.

A small, triumphant smile played on her lips. These were victories, small but significant. They were testaments to her strength, her resilience, and her unwavering determination to heal.

The book also offered a gentle nudge to forgive herself. Not forgive Michael, for his actions were inexcusable, but to forgive herself for the mistakes she might have made, for the times she doubted her own worth.

This self-forgiveness wasn't about condoning the abuse; it was about releasing the burden of guilt and shame, and stepping forward with a lighter heart.

Sitting on a park bench, Amelia pulled out her journal. The crisp autumn air seemed to mirror the clarity in her mind. She began to write, pouring out her emotions, her fears, and her newfound hope. "*I forgive myself for trusting the wrong person,*" she wrote, the words flowing freely. "*I forgive myself for the times I doubted my strength. I am worthy of love, respect, and a future filled with happiness.*"

Tears welled up in her eyes, but this time they were tears of release, of letting go. As she closed her journal, a sense of peace settled over her. The road ahead might still hold uncertainties, but she faced them with a newfound courage.

The park was abuzz with activity – children chasing pigeons, couples strolling hand-in-hand, a group of friends sharing laughter and conversation. Amelia watched them, a flicker of longing tugging at her heart.

Then, a memory surfaced – a forgotten dream tucked away in a dusty corner of her mind. She'd always wanted to learn how to play the guitar, the soulful melody a balm for the soul. A spark ignited within her.

Without a moment's hesitation, Amelia stood up, the fallen leaves crunching under her feet. She knew what she had to do. This wasn't just about celebrating victories; it was about embracing the future, a future filled with her passions, her dreams, and the possibility of love that felt safe and respectful.

Walking towards the nearest music store, Amelia felt a lightness in her step she hadn't experienced in weeks.

Week 7 wasn't just about the end of Breakup Bootcamp; it was a new beginning, a chance to write a new chapter in the story of her life, a chapter filled with hope, possibility, and the exhilarating uncertainty of what lay ahead.

Amelia's story might resonate with you in a powerful way if you've recently emerged from a difficult breakup, especially one marked by emotional abuse.

Perhaps you, too, are grappling with the lingering effects of the relationship, questioning your own worth and struggling to find reasons to celebrate. Maybe the idea of moving forward feels daunting, the path ahead shrouded in uncertainty.

Regardless of your specific circumstances, Amelia's journey offers valuable life lessons and takeaways that can empower you to celebrate your victories, forgive yourself, and embrace the exciting possibilities that lie ahead.

Life Lessons:

1. Healing is a Journey, Not a Destination: Don't expect to wake up one day completely healed.

Healing is a process with ups and downs, moments of triumph followed by setbacks.

2. Self-Compassion is Key: Forgive yourself for the mistakes you might have made during the relationship. Focus on self-love and acceptance as you move forward.

3. The Power of Gratitude: Take time each day to reflect on the things you're grateful for, big or small. Gratitude can shift your perspective and boost your overall well-being.

4. Embrace Your Dreams: Reconnect with passions and dreams you might have neglected during the relationship. Pursue these dreams as a way to reclaim your sense of self and create a fulfilling future.

5. The Future Holds Possibility: Letting go of the past opens the door to new beginnings.

Key Takeaways:

1. You Are Stronger Than You Think: The challenges you've overcome have made you stronger and more resilient. Believe in your own strength and ability to heal.

2. Celebrate Every Milestone: Acknowledge your progress, no matter how small. Every step forward is a victory on your healing journey.

3. Release the Burden of Guilt: Forgive yourself for trusting the wrong person.

4. Your Life is Yours to Design: This is your chance to create a life that reflects your true self, your values, and your dreams.

5. Love Will Find You Again: Healthy, fulfilling love exists. When you're ready, open your heart to the possibility of new connections.

Remember, healing after a breakup, especially one involving emotional abuse, takes time and dedication. Be patient with yourself, celebrate your victories, and embrace the exciting possibilities that await you.

The only person you are destined to become is the person you decide to be. Choose to be strong, resilient, and open to the love and happiness you deserve.

Gratitude Jar

Every day, write down something you're grateful for. Revisiting these notes on a challenging day can shift your perspective and boost your mood.

Gratitude Jar

Every day, write down something you're grateful for. Revisiting these notes on a challenging day can shift your perspective and boost your mood.

Gratitude Jar

Every day, write down something you're grateful for. Revisiting these notes on a challenging day can shift your perspective and boost your mood.

Self-Reflection Questions:

What kind of future do I envision for myself?

What are some of my fears and anxieties about moving forward? How can I challenge these fears and approach the future with greater confidence?

What are some dreams or passions I've neglected during the relationship? How can I start incorporating them into my life again?

Self-Reflection Questions:

What are some areas where I need to practice self-compassion?

Self-Reflection Questions:

What are some of the small victories I've achieved on my healing journey?
How can I celebrate these accomplishments?

CONCLUSION

A year had passed since Amelia had embarked on her healing journey with Breakup Bootcamp. Ten weeks that felt like a lifetime, a whirlwind of emotions, and a profound transformation.

The ache of the past relationship had dulled to a distant memory, a reminder of her strength and resilience. The emotional abuse, the manipulation, the constant walking on eggshells – those were shadows of a bygone era.

The past year had been a testament to her unwavering spirit. She'd reconnected with cherished friends, their laughter a balm to her soul. She'd thrown herself into her passion for music, the soulful melody of her guitar a constant companion. Most importantly, she'd cultivated a deep sense of self-love and acceptance.

Looking back, Amelia couldn't help but marvel at the progress she'd made. The woman staring back at her from the mirror was no longer a victim, but a survivor, a thriver. Her eyes shone with a newfound confidence, a quiet strength that resonated from within.

Breakup Bootcamp hadn't just equipped her with tools and strategies; it had empowered her to rewrite her own narrative. The book's final message echoed in her mind: "A brighter future awaits."

And indeed, the future stretched before her, an uncharted territory filled with exciting possibilities. She wasn't sure what love or happiness might look like, but she was open to the possibilities. She craved a connection built on mutual respect, trust, and genuine affection.

This year, Amelia made a conscious decision to stop waiting for love to find her. She decided to focus on creating a life that felt fulfilling, a life that reflected her values and aspirations. She enrolled in a creative writing course, her fingers dancing across the keyboard as she poured her heart into stories. She volunteered at a local animal shelter, her heart overflowing with love as she walked the abandoned dogs.

Life wasn't perfect, of course. There were still moments of doubt, fleeting anxieties about the future. But Amelia had learned to navigate these challenges with grace and self-compassion. She had her support system – her friends, her therapist, and the unwavering belief in herself.

One evening, while walking her dog Luna in the park, Amelia bumped into a man with a kind smile and eyes that held a hint of warmth. They struck up a conversation, their laughter blending with the rustling leaves. It was an unexpected encounter, a spark of connection that ignited a flicker of hope within her.

As they walked along the park path, Amelia realized something profound. Love wasn't something she had to chase; it was something that unfolded organically when she least expected it. The most important love story, after all, was the one she was writing with herself – a story of healing, growth, and self-discovery.

The year may have begun with the remnants of a broken heart, but it was ending on a note of hope, possibility, and a heart brimming with love for herself. Amelia knew, deep down, that the brightest chapters of her life were yet to be written.

Amelia's story might resonate deeply with you if you're nearing the end of your own healing journey after a difficult breakup, especially one marked by emotional abuse.

Perhaps you, too, stand on the precipice of a new beginning, a future filled with hope and possibility. Maybe you wonder if the ache of the past will ever truly fade, and if you'll ever be open to love again.

THANK YOU

You turn the final page, a quiet sense of closure washes over you. Ten weeks of facing the raw emotions, the buried pain, and the slow, steady climb towards healing. This journey, chronicled within the pages of *"Overcoming Breakup Grief,"* wasn't just about surviving a difficult breakup; it was about rediscovering yourself.

Perhaps, like Amelia, you too stared into the abyss of heartbreak, the shards of a shattered relationship leaving you feeling lost and alone. Maybe the emotional abuse cast a long shadow, whispering doubts and threatening to dim your inner light. But within these pages, you found a beacon of hope, a gentle guide leading you through the darkness.

There were moments of tears, of course. Tears of anger, of sadness, of the deep grief that accompanies the loss of a relationship. But amidst the tears, there were also moments of epiphany, of rediscovering your strength, and the unwavering resilience of the human spirit.

As you close the book, a single word resonates within you: Thank you. Thank you for the journey, for the support, and for the gentle nudge towards a brighter future.

ABOUT THE AUTHOR

The author of "Overcoming Breakup Grief" isn't just a writer; She is a fellow traveler on the path of healing. Her own experiences with heartbreak and abuse fueled a passion to create a resource for others navigating similar challenges.

This book is born from empathy, from a deep understanding of the emotional turmoil that accompanies a difficult breakup, especially one marked by emotional abuse. It's a testament to the power of vulnerability, of sharing your story to help others heal.

The author remains shrouded in a veil of anonymity, their focus solely on empowering you, the reader. Her voice, however, resonates throughout the book, a warm and compassionate hand guiding you through the ten-week program. This isn't goodbye; it's a new beginning.